MASTER OF ALL YOU SURVEY:

How to use surveys to improve organizations, teams & leaders

David Chaudron, PhD

Organized Change Publications

Master of All you Survey: How to use surveys to improve organizations, teams & leaders.
Copyright ©2006 by Organized Change Corporation.
Manufactured in the United States of America.

Published by Organized Change Publications, 5663 Balboa Ave. #171 San Diego CA 92111.
(858) 694-8191. First edition.

Cover Design: Oxana Gusak, Visual Arts Group
Layout and Illustrations: Kelly Mayerick and Matthew Torch

Library of Congress Cataloging-in-Publication Data
Chaudron, David, 1959-

Master of all you survey: How to use surveys to improve organizations,
teams and leaders / David Chaudron.-- 1st ed. p. cm.

Includes bibliographical references and index.
ISBN-13: 978-0-9723626-6-5 (alk. paper) 1. Organizational change. 2. Surveys.
3. Employee attitude surveys. 4. Employer attitude surveys. I. Title.
HD58.8.C4643 2006
658.30072'3--dc22
2006002219

TABLE OF CONTENTS

Table of Charts and Illustrations   vii

About the Author   ix

Special Thanks   xi

Preface   xiii

Master of all you Survey   1

1   The Whats, WhyFors, HowComes, and What to Keep in Mind   3

2   Performance Measurement and the Balanced Scorecard   9

3   How to Plan, Develope and Act on Survey Date   13

Focus: Organization   27

4   Assessing and Improving Your Organization: Symptoms, Diagnosis, and Cures   29

5   Case Study: Survey-Based Organizational Change   33

Focus: Team   **43**

Diagnosing Team Problems   45

Case Study: How Not To Use A Team   51

Focus: Improving Leaders   **57**

Giving Feedback on Management Style: 59
The Three Degrees of 360° Feedback

Acknowledgement and Suggested Readings   **69**

Table of Charts and Illustrations

Assessment and Measurement
The Balanced Scorecard   5
Concern-Solution Matrix   19
Kinds of Scales to Use   22
Survey Data Before Organizational Change   36
Weighting Matrix for Selecting Employees   39
  to Fill Open Positions
Survey Data Before and After Organizational Change   41

Focus: Improving Leaders
Result of the Data Collection   53
Average of Responses   64
Survey Items   65

SPECIAL THANKS

Thanks go to many people, who helped both emotionally and technically. Thanks to Tom Meehl, Wayne Groesbeck, Ron Kenner and Kelly Mayerick for editing and formatting this book. Thanks also to Cathi Stevenson for her great work on the cover design. It is a much better product for their efforts and made me see problems with my writing I wouldn't have discovered. Thanks to Fred Brauer and Ozzie Gontang, whose initial advice and assistance proved invaluable.

My thanks also go to our customers at Organized Change, who provided so much learning for me over these 20 years and also provided the money to pay the mortgage.

PREFACE

"We've heard we might have a morale problem. Survey the employees and find out if anything is going on."

"It's time for our annual employee survey."

"Find out why we've had our third sexual harassment complaint this year."

"That nice consultant called again. He said you had wanted to have a survey about now."

The words above fill you, at best, with anticipation; more likely with anxiety; and just possibly with dread.

There are many reasons for these feelings: Opening a can of worms is not your favorite pastime; surveys usually involve the intersection of number crunching and people's perceptions; not an easy task. You know about the horror stories of management collecting all that information and doing nothing with it.

If all this sounds familiar, it's because we've heard all of these (and a few more) in our twenty-five years of experience helping clients on five continents. Rest assured that although your fears, concerns and hopes are legitimate, there are ways and methods of using surveys that meet your needs; and a survey can be a driver of action, not a passenger with paperwork. This book is designed to give you the outlines of the actions to accomplish just that.

MASTER OF ALL YOU SURVEY:

How to use surveys to improve organizations, teams & leaders

1

THE WHATS, WHYFORS, HOWCOMES, AND WHAT TO KEEP IN MIND

Besides someone more powerful than you telling you to do so, there are four main reasons for making assessments and surveys:

1) To find out what is happening and act on what you find. This is akin to turning on a flashlight in a darkened alley. You never know quite what to expect. However, for those brave enough to turn on the light, the problems only hinted at in the shadows can be forthrightly dealt with. Such an enterprise, especially when you are dealing with more subjective measures such as organizational climate, team morale, or management style, is especially problematic. Translating this information into action helpful to the company's success is an additional issue that many fail to address. See 'Planning and Analyzing Employee Surveys' to understand the decisions and steps necessary to conduct and successfully act on surveys and the data they generate.

2) To create a baseline. An organization may want to create a comparison so as to describe where it is now on organizational climate, job satisfaction, morale, etc., before management makes organizational changes. A note of caution here. Many people confuse a "baseline" with a "benchmark." A "baseline" is a starting point of measurement. However, a "benchmark" is a standard of excellence for a particular process, outcome, or type of organization. Baselines involve your own company, while benchmarks involve gathering objective information about how an organization with world-class processes produces its goods and services.

3) To evaluate if change has occurred. The consequence of establishing a baseline is that you need to re-measure to determine if there have been significant changes in what you are measuring. Whether this measurement is done continuously, periodically or only one time, this reassessment allows you to measure the effects of organizational change.

4) To assess the measurement system itself. When implementing organizational change, we often focus on measuring our own efforts or on the effects of a particular organizational change. However, when an organization considers more fundamental change, new issues arise. What measures of success should the organization have- is measuring profitability the sole criterion for a company? Our answer is a resounding "No!" We have found that an approach called the 'Balanced Scorecard' provides excellent insight into a company (See the chapter: 'Performance Measurement and the Balanced Scorecard.') Surveys can be one component of an organization's measurement system.

Regardless of why your organization wants to measure, six questions need to be considered when thinking about surveys:

1) Which do we need, an assessment and/or or a measurement system? What is a survey anyway?

An assessment is a one-time evaluation of an issue, concern, problem or area of interest that can use multiple methods of gathering information. An employee survey is an assessment that gathers subjective information such as the feelings, opinions, beliefs and values of the people that work in your organization. A measurement system, regardless of whether it is using subjective (opinions, feelings and perceptions) or objective information (rates of return, % defects, etc.) , involves repeatedly measuring something, reviewing the data and acting on what is found. Though these terms may differ, they all must be reliable and valid. If surveys are done systematically and are integrated into the other measures of performance, they become part of the measurement system as well.

ABOUT THE AUTHOR

David Chaudron, Ph.D., managing partner for Organized Change™ Consultancy, brings more than 25 years of experience assisting firms in their efforts to improve effectiveness, quality, and employee involvement. His efforts have included practical designs for major change efforts, strategic planning, reengineering, survey development, team building, Total Quality Management, one-on-one coaching, and employee selection systems.

He has worked with manufacturing, financial services, banking, software, electronics, petroleum, including government and international organizations. His experience includes:

* Developing and managing implementation strategies for major organizations.

* Assessing organizational climate, group climate and management.

* Developing strategic plans using scenario planning.

* Designing, developing, and delivering materials for training Six Sigma advisors.

* Conducting management training in the United States, Europe, the Mid East and South America.

* Conducting team building, including cross-national teambuilding sessions with middle and upper management.

* Coaching senior management on management style and interpersonal relations with subordinates using 360-degree feedback.

- Developing and enhancing processes for selection and recruitment.

- Conducting job analyses to define career paths aligned to company vision.

He is also adjunct Professor at the Alliant International University, teaching strategic planning, change management, personnel selection, and Six Sigma. He has written more than 25 articles on organizational change and assessment and is a speaker for the International Training Center (http://www.itc-group.org), an organization that provides monthly management training to more than 35,000 people in North and South America.

He may be reached via email at *dgc@organizedchange.com*, or through the Organized Change™ website at *http://www.organizedchange.com*.

2) How do we collect our data so that it is actionable? How do we translate the data we collect into action? While much can be done to construct a survey so that it is more actionable (See 'Planning and Analyzing Employee Surveys'), the rest of the answer concerns how best to implement organizational change in a way that increases effectiveness and minimizes resistance. One way of accomplishing this is to involve powerful employees in the survey development and change effort. For an example of this, you might read our case study on organizational change on our Focus: Organization section.

3) At what layer (organizational, team, or individual) do I start? Where is the problem located?

These are questions that for which people assume an answer without much thought. An organization can be viewed as a whole, and thus questions that can be asked include those on organizational climate and culture, pay and benefits, etc. An organization can also be viewed as many subgroups or teams and where questions include those on teamwork, cooperation, sharing, openness to comment, organization of work, etc. It also can be viewed as a collection of individuals where there are relevant questions about a person's job, such as clarity of duties, job satisfaction, commitment to the organization, and sufficient authority. If the individual(s) is a supervisor or manager, questions include leadership, encouragement to improve, listening skills, etc.

The type of problem (organizational, team/group, or individual) the severity of the problem and the problem's scope (how widespread it is) interact with each other. This can significantly affect what techniques are best used to help solve the problems you discover.

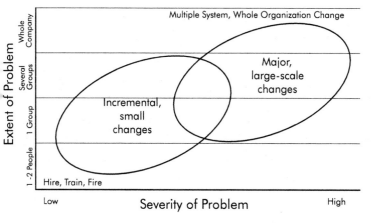

As you can see in the above illustration, if the problems your survey identifies only affect a few individuals and the severity of the problem is low, you might put that person into a training program, or perhaps shift this worker into another job. On the other hand, if your survey reveals that there are severe problems across the organization, then a multiple system or whole organizational change might be required.

If, for example, it turns out that severe problems with teamwork exist in only one group, then an offsite meeting might be useful to allow the group to discuss and problem solve around these issues. On the other hand, if your survey reveals teamwork issues across the whole organization, then teambuilding merely one group at a time would only address part of the problem. The systems, procedures, and hiring problems that caused such wide-ranging concerns should be addressed as well.

This distinction between the layers and how to act on each one of them is so important, the book is organized that way. The section, 'Focus: Organization' deals with organization-wide change. Similarly, 'Focus: Teams' deals with the team layer, and the 'Focus: Individual' talks about the individual layer, specifically how to use 360° degree feedback to improve management style. Each section includes a chapter with more information on how to setup and diagnose such problems, and includes case studies from our clients.

4) How do we know something has changed? Have we setup our data collection so we can find this out? The consequence of establishing a baseline is that you need to re-measure to find out if there have been significant changes in what you are measuring. Whether this measurement is done continuously, periodically, or only one time, this reassessment allows you to measure effects of organizational change.

A fuller explanation of all the methods that can be used to find if what you did has any effect is beyond the scope of this book. Suffice it say at the moment there are three main methods to find answer to this question: experimental designs, quasi-experimental designs, and time-series designs.

Experimental designs involve control and experimental groups, to which people are randomly assigned. The control group continues unchanged while the various experimental groups are introduced to differing conditions. The resulting data are analyzed using analysis of variance, also known as ANOVA. True experiments are difficult to

perform in organizations because employees are not randomly assigned to supervisors, functions, or their work location.

You can use quasi-experimental designs when you have roughly equivalent groups, such as multiple facilities that accomplish much of the same work. There are control and experimental groups, and the data are analyzed in much the same way.

Time-series designs single groups or organizations and measures effects over time. The types of designs can be as simple as the pre-post design used in the Focus: Organization section, or as complex as a Box-Jenkins time series analysis with an intervention component. (Now that you know this, impress your friends!) For much more information than you probably care to know, see the Cook & Campbell (1979), McCleary & Hay (1980) and Chaudron (1992) in the Acknowledgements and Suggested Readings section.

5) If and how should we use outside resources to help us?

Perspective, objectivity, and confidentiality. It is all too easy for employees to think their company spies on them, reviewing every email, voicemail and conversation. The problem can be avoided by having an outside party conduct the survey, since the data can be collected anonymously. In addition, outside resources can provide the perspective of other companies' experiences; perspectives seen as not coming from the management team (perhaps) perceived as the cause of problem.

Expertise and experience in the process. A survey often involves a combination of planning, logistics, multiple languages, degree of survey customization, integration into existing change efforts and detailed statistical analysis. The success of your survey effort will depend on how these factors are dealt with.

Resources, including survey content. Consulting firms have access to their own content, in addition to public sources. This content can often be customized to a client's unique needs. Their software tools are often customized to deal with employee surveys and can handle the varied needs, including multiple languages, unique demographic breakouts, graphing and charting, etc.

Because our consultants are nice, caring people. We really are.

2

PERFORMANCE MEASUREMENT AND THE BALANCED SCORECARD

Using the Balanced Scorecard to Combine Viewpoints of Company Success

While a variety of chapters here and elsewhere talk about measurement and assessment of particular things (employee opinions, company strengths, specific projects, etc.),we need to ask a larger question. How should a company measure its overall success? In the long term, to develop good measures of company morale while keeping a broken system of company success is a recipe for failure.

Described below, in brief, is a way of measuring company success and encouraging alignment between an organization's strategy, measures and all of the actions taken to achieve them.

Problems with Just One Measure of Success

If you were to ask most anyone how they would measure company performance, they might give you a funny look and say, "How much money the company makes, of course! Isn't that obvious?" To a certain extent, they are right. Profitability, gross revenues, return on capital, etc., are the critical "bottom line" kind of results that companies must deliver to survive. Unfortunately, if senior management only focuses on the financial health of the organization, several unfortunate consequences arise. One is that financial measures are lagging indicators of success. This means that how high or low these numbers go depends on a wide variety of events (discussed later) that may have occurred months or years before, events over which you have no immediate control in the present. Being in a plane falling from the sky is a bad time to realize you should have done routine maintenance, and oh, by the way, filled it with gasoline!

Another consequence of only focusing on financial measures is that these have nothing to do directly with the customers who use your organization's product or service. Decisions may be made that help your organization financially yet hurt your long-term relationships with your customers, those who may eventually reduce their purchases or drop out altogether. Most of us have found ourselves paying for car repairs that we need but that we know we are paying too much for; we also know that we will never go back to that service station again.

Instead of such a short-sighted, after-the-fact view of company performance we need a more comprehensive view with an equal emphasis on outcome measures (the financial measures or lagging indicators), measures that will tell us how well the company is doing now (current indicators) and measures of how it might do in the future (leading indicators)

To accomplish this, use the balanced scorecard method of measuring company success.

What is the Balanced Scorecard?

The balanced scorecard is a remedy for this kind of problem. First of all, the balanced scorecard is a way of:

- ❊ Measuring organizational, business unit or department success

- ❊ Balancing long-term and short-term actions

- ❊ Balancing different measures of success

  - Financial

  - Customer

  - Internal Operations

  - Human Resource Systems & Development(learning and growth)

- ❊ A way of linking strategy to measures to action

Four Kinds of Measures

Under the balanced scorecard system, financial measures are the outcome but do not offer a good indication of what is or will be going on in the organization. Measures of customer satisfaction, growth and retention are the current indicator of company performance, while internal operations (efficiency, speed, reducing non-value added work, minimizing quality problems) and human resource systems and development are leading indicators of company performance.

Context and Strategy

Just as financial measures have to be put in context, so does measurement itself. Without a tie to a company strategy, more importantly, as *the measure* of company strategy, the balanced scorecard (or BSC) is useless. A mission, strategy and objectives must be defined; measures of that strategy (the BSC) must be agreed to; and actions need to be performed for a measurement system to be fully effective. Otherwise, to use an American expression, the company is all dressed up but has nowhere to go.

Finding the Causes (Drivers) of Success

Once the company mission, strategy and measures have been defined and agreed upon, the next step is to understand fully the drivers (causes) behind movement (up and down) of your balanced scorecard. Without the specific knowledge of what drivers will affect your scorecard, your organization might well spend much time, money and effort and yet achieve very little.

These drivers fall into four categories:

* Environmental - those factors outside the influence of your organization, such as governmental regulations, the economic cycle, local, national and global politics, etc.

* Organizational - systems inside the organization such as company strategy, human resource systems, policies, procedures, organizational structure, pay, etc.

* Group or departmental - work processes, group relationships, work responsibilities, work assignments

* Individual - personality, management style, skills, behaviors.

For more information, see the references for the Balanced Scorecard in the *'Acknowledgements and Suggested Readings'* at the end of this section.

3

How to Plan, Develop and Act on Survey Data

Planning the Employee Survey

One of the major reasons why organizations don't receive the benefit from surveys is that they don't plan them well. Planning not only makes for less stress while analyzing the survey but helps define assumptions and expectations about what you want to achieve. The following are good "rules of thumb" for planning your survey, followed by a few more suggestions to help analyze that mound of paper in front of you when the returns are in.

Keep the Data Anonymous, But Communicate the Actions.

Organizations often keep survey information anonymous and confidential to increase the accuracy of the data received. This rule of thumb is usually a good idea, but can also have its drawbacks. Among these drawbacks is the uncertainty of what to do with survey comments that allege illegal actions or violations of company procedures. Acting on such comments may violate the confidentiality of the respondents. Additionally, confidentiality can lead to inaction by those who need change the most, as the following story illustrates.

We had conducted an employee survey for an aerospace client who had decided that accusations concerning individual behavior would be noted but not acted upon. This was done to ensure the survey would not become a witch hunt but would rather focus on organization-wide issues. Unfortunately, in the written comments collected, there were accusations of a married manager getting a single woman pregnant and rewarding her with a promotion. These accusations, if true, were a violation of company policy and normally would be investigated. However, as a result of the confidentiality restriction, the information was not directly acted upon.

As you can see, investigating specific accusations can be a problem. The organization has a choice of ignoring the problem or of trying to find out more information in focus groups. This randomly selected group of people can be asked if certain allegations are true, and what additional information they might have. These sessions need to be held with the utmost confidentiality by a person of good reputation working for no one in the group.

Don't Look for What You Already See.

Many organizations believe they understand their problems, and call in consultants to work out the details. This is a self-fulfilling prophecy. If an organization investigates only subject 'X', it will only get back information on subject X. Management overlooks other issues of major concern, as the following example shows.

An organization changed its telephone system and hired a consultant to determine the company's training needs. After talking with the users of the new equipment, the consultant realized that it was not ignorance that was causing the organization's telecommunication problems. Instead, it was a management and cultural problem.

Organizations can get around this problem somewhat by using a broad-spectrum survey at the beginning of the effort, then ask specific questions later. Other ways around this problem are discussed in the next section.

Use Multiple Survey Methods.

Using multiple techniques to ask about the same kind of information is a hallmark of good information gathering. Any surveying technique has its weaknesses. For example, numerical surveys (where survey items are rating on a scale of one to five) are easy to score. However, the specific wording of the question may not exactly apply, and may miss getting to the heart of the matter. In addition, numerical surveys, especially those that ask a narrow set of questions, only allow survey takers to be asked a limited set of topics. An organization may miss discovering important issues because the questions weren't asked.

On the other hand, open-ended questionnaires have less of this problem. This is because questions are less precise and so get richer information from the survey taker. Unfortunately, the more open-ended the questionnaire the harder it is to score. Whoever summarizes written comments injects one's own opinions into the rating process, something that does not happen with numerical surveys.

Focus groups offer potentially the richest source of information for gathering information. This is true in part because the leader of focus groups can ask clarifying questions. However, because verbal information is such a rich source it is more difficult to summarize and classify than are written surveys. In addition, employees in focus groups and individual interviews lose anonymity.

My recommendation is to use not one approach but, if possible, all of them. Using one method simply doesn't cover all the bases. Focus groups and individual interviews are useful at the very beginning of the survey effort to find broad areas of concern. Open-ended survey questions and numerical surveys can pinpoint specific issues and allow employees to express their concerns anonymously. Use focus groups again to get feedback on specific issues or recommendations.

Such information nowadays doesn't have to be gathered via paper and pencil. Programs are available that allow employees to take the survey at their own computers, whether as a standalone program or whether they have Internet access via the World Wide Web. Our experience has shown that these methods produce more reliable results.

Decide How to Analyze Data Before You Gather It.

One manager of a manufacturing organization developed a preliminary survey to assess the effects of their 'delayering' of the department. He sent it to other managers, wishing to get their feedback about the questions he developed. Instead of getting feedback about the questions, he received more than 50 filled-out surveys! As a result of this unexpected response, he had not decided what graphs, charts and analysis he needed. It took a staff assistant many long hours to change the data into a workable form.

When creating surveys, decide how to analyze, chart and graph the data before employees complete them. This approach avoids bias when there is no set procedure for analysis, and reduces last-minute panic when the data comes flooding in. After developing the survey and if you remain uncertain about the analysis, I recommend giving the preliminary survey to a sample of people who are similar to employees. To make analysis easier, use this sample of individuals to fine-tune questions, decide how to analyze the data, and change the questions.

Decide on Your Sampling Plan and How to 'Break Out' the Data.

Many organizations survey their employees, usually once a year. Two problems arise from this practice. First, because the organization surveys only once one can't distinguish between flukes and trends. Only by surveying multiple times a year, using a sample of employees, can an organization distinguish between special, one-time events and ongoing concerns. Second, because employees can behave differently just before survey time. This 'Hawthorne effect,' where employees temporarily change their behavior based on expectations, can mask underlying problems. A reverse Hawthorne effect can also occur, where employees worsen their behavior and exaggerate their responses on the survey.

When deciding on a sampling plan, decide how to break out (stratify) the data before distributing the survey. Common breakouts include such matters as how staff employees feel compared to line employees, how each department answered the survey, or how male respondents compared to female ones. These breakouts can help pinpoint employee groups concerned about a particular issue. However, survey authors and analysts often make the mistake of using multiple 't' tests to determine whether more than two group means are statistically different from one another. Because these sample means are non-independent, it's not easy to determine or interpret the level of significance. More appropriate statistics that avoid this problem are multiple comparisons, discriminant analysis, or logistic regression. For more information on these techniques, please see the '*Acknowledgements and Suggested Readings*' at the end of this chapter.

Because these breakouts are easy to do with today's computers, organizations can create graphs and charts for their own sake. The greater the number of breakouts, the more employees must be surveyed at any given time. Otherwise, samples can be so small that the survey data are unreliable. As with any sampling method, the smaller the sample of employees the greater the uncertainty that the sample's statistics will match population parameters. One can reduce this uncertainty by increasing the sample size and using more reliable and varied methods of measurement. Of course this is typically accomplished at the cost of a more time-consuming survey. As with all sampling plans, survey analysts should evaluate survey statistics in light of survey results and change their sampling accordingly.

Involve Employees, Especially Powerful Ones in the Survey Effort.

Organizations can survey their employees, accurately assess their needs, and still find much resistance to change. One way to lessen this problem is to involve, formally and informally, powerful employees into the group that develops or selects the survey, distributes and analyzes the results, develops recommendations, and implements solutions. Such employees can include management, union officials, and elected representatives of departments. These employees act as spokespersons for the groups they represent, communicate events to these groups, and provide vital information to the survey process. One group included a vice president, a director, a manager, two engineers, two supervisors, two from administrative support, and two inspectors who represented employees.

Never Survey Without Acting.

Management can survey their employees to assess working conditions out of curiosity, or to relieve their anxieties about everything being "all right." However, surveys raise expectations by those who take them, and those they tell. When expectations of change remain unfulfilled, employees can become more demoralized than before the survey.

Management might ask, "What if we survey our employees, and can't [or won't] do anything about their problems?" These concerns are frequent when distrust is high between management and the rest of the employees, or where historically they have not gotten along. On one hand, such statements can be an excuse for inaction, but on the other, they raise a point.

Even before the survey authors create the survey or gather the data, management must decide which actions are possible and which are not. When employees raise concerns, management needs to communicate that they understand these concerns. If management cannot immediately solve these issues, employees must know this. At the minimum, management must communicate survey data and their response. Preferably, management should answer concerns and act on them.

Include the Survey Process in the Normal Business Planning Cycle.

One way to influence an organization is to become part of its planning cycle - its goals, objectives, and budgets. Employee involvement efforts can achieve this by scheduling survey events so recommendations are ready the month before budget planning sessions. To accomplish this, schedule backwards. For example, if budgets are due in June, present survey recommendations in May and develop them in April. Analyze the survey recommendations in March, and distribute the survey (assuming a 'one shot' survey) in February. Determine the survey ground rules in January, and form the survey group in December. By scheduling this way, surveys deliver the maximum 'punch' possible.

Without such planning, management is more likely to respond to survey and employee suggestions with, "That's nice," and then follow up with "Sounds like a good idea. Where is the money to pay for it?"

Create Clear, Specific Actions From the Survey Data.

"We must communicate more," and "We must change people's attitudes" are often the recommendations that come from surveys. Unfortunately, these platitudes do little to fix the problems that survey responses communicate. Listed in the following table are some possible concerns raised by employees, and a brief summary of what might be done with each issue.

Employee Concerns	Possible Solution
Fairness of promotions	Change selection, promotion procedures, who decision-makers are
Fairness of pay system	Gainsharing, flexible benefits plan
Performance reviews	Reward groups instead of individuals, change rating process
Career development	Create career ladders, clarify job descriptions, create mentoring systems, pay for knowledge
Communication	Bulletin boards, all-hands meetings, company videos, E-mail, focus groups
Empowerment	Delegate specific authority and decisions to employees
Inter-group warfare, between-department communication management style	Inter-group teambuilding, restructure by product or customer instead of functionally 360° feedback, management training

Concern-Solution Matrix

Clearly Communicate the Survey Process, Recommendations and Actions.

Communication is a crucial ingredient in every phase of the survey process. Organizations must inform employees about survey planning, data collection, and implementation plans. Without this communication, employees who would otherwise support the survey become confused, frustrated, and eventually complacent. Loss of this critical mass of support may eventually doom whatever changes the company implements.

Use Surveys With Good Reliability and Validity.

Validity is determined by how well a survey measures what it should. This usually means measuring each survey topic with several questions, and in several ways. It means raising at least three questions, preferably five on each survey topic, and asking similar questions during interviews and focus groups. To minimize unclear or missing questions, review the survey's validity by comparing it to existing methods of gathering information.

Reliability is determined by how consistent the survey is over time, and by the consistency of survey items with each other. If a survey is unreliable, survey statistics will move up and down without employee opinions really changing. What may appear to be a significant change over time may be owing to the unreliability of the survey methods used.

If you've created or changed a survey, determine its reliability on groups similar to your employees. Even if you don't change the survey, check and see what reliability and validity studies have been done. Even if you don't change the survey at all, it is a good idea to test the survey on a sample of your employees. It's worse than useless for your organization to hand out a survey and receive information of unknown worth.

Developing the Survey and Analyzing the Results

In the first part of our chapter, we talked about how to properly plan and implement employee surveys, and how to integrate them into organizational change. This chapter will focus on how to develop the survey itself and how to make it a useful, reliable measurement tool of organizational change.

Develop Items.

It is generally best not to start out with individual items for your survey, but to develop broad categories (subscales) of questions. Then generate at least three questions per category. Three to five questions are needed as a minimum for consistency and reliability.

For example, let's say that the survey authors decide to measure "the effectiveness of a supervisor's listening skills." Most survey authors would simply ask one question, such as "How would you rate your supervisor's listening skills?"

This is the equivalent of a one-legged horse: it looks funny, and doesn't stand on its own. Instead, make 3-4 questions in the "effectiveness of a supervisor's listening skills" category, such as:

1) How would you rate your supervisor's listening skills?

2) How comfortable do I feel about telling my supervisor about ideas for doing my job better?

3) How often does my supervisor listen to and act on what I say?

4) How well does my supervisor understand my point of view?

Repeat this exercise for every category to be measured.

Format the Survey and Develop Instructions.

Survey formats should be as clear and simple as possible and should make clear to the respondent how to answer each question. As much as possible, reduce the chance of 'crossover' errors where employees mean to answer one question but accidentally answer another. For surveys with numbers to circle, boxes to check, etc., make sure that questions 1) either have ellipses (...) or an underscoring line from the end of the question to the numbers to be circled, or 2) formatting (bold text, italics, different type sizes, etc.) that clearly highlight what question goes with what answer.

One thing you should definitely not do, especially the first time you use a survey, is list the survey items by group so that, for example, questions 1,2 3,4 5, all refer to a supervisor's listening skills, and questions 6,7,8,9, and 10 all refer to management's responsiveness to change. Do not put 'headlines' on the survey telling everyone how you have lumped together the survey items. This defeats the purpose of factor analysis, as described below, and increases the 'halo effect,' the tendency of employees to answer questions the same way.

Develop Survey Scales & Avoid the Agree-Disagree Type.

This has nothing to do with rust, alligators or how much weight you've gained since the holidays. Instead, it's deciding how to ask employees to react to questions. Many people use "agree/disagree" scales, so people give answers such as:

1. I like ice cream
- ⁕ Strongly agree
- ⁕ Agree
- ⁕ Neutral
- ⁕ Disagree
- ⁕ Strongly disagree

2. I hate ice cream
- ⁕ Strongly agree
- ⁕ Agree
- ⁕ Neutral
- ⁕ Disagree
- ⁕ Strongly disagree

Unfortunately this kind of scale has many problems. Firstly, studies have shown that these scales suffer from 'response set bias,' the tendency of employees to agree with both the statement and its exact opposite, as in the case above. Secondly, analyzing these kinds of statements is very difficult. If I strongly disagree with the statement, "I like ice cream," what does that mean? It could mean that I hate ice cream or it could mean that I don't like it; I love it to death. There is no way of telling what these employees intended. The ambiguity decreases the reliability of the survey you are developing.

Frequency	1. My supervisor gives me feedback on my performance	Never	Once or Twice	Sometimes	Often	Always
Intensity	1. My supervisor actively listens to what I say	To no extent	To a little extent	To a modest extent	To some extent	To a great extent
Duration	1. My supervisor keeps eye contact with me during my performance review	At no time at all	For a little time	For much of the time	For a long time	Continuously
Need for improvement	1. How promotions are handled in my department	Needs no improvement	Needs a little improvement	Needs some improvement	Needs much improvement	Needs drastic improvement

Kinds of Scales to Use

Instead use frequency, intensity, duration or need for change/need for improvement. Specifically, these scales would be something like this:

Another kind of "scaling" to avoid if possible is "ipsative" or "forced-choice" scoring. The assumption behind this kind of scoring is that if you receive a high score on one survey category, you must receive a low score on other survey categories. While it's often true that high scores on one category (focus on task, for example) correlate somewhat with low scores on another (focus on people, for example), you shouldn't force this by your scoring method.

Send Out a Sample and Correct Any Problems.

As noted earlier, after you've developed the initial draft of the survey, try it out on a sample of people similar to those who will ultimately take the survey. Conducting this sample satisfies several objectives: 1) it allows feedback on the clarity of questions, 2) it allows you to practice the 'pitch' to survey takers, 3) it allows statistics (see *factor analysis* below) to be produced that will tell how reliable your survey is and how to group your questions into categories, and 4) it allows practice of the step-by-step logistical sequence needed to disseminate, collect and enter the data of the survey into the computer.

Collect Your Data.

This is not as simple as it seems. To maximize the rate of return, you must carefully encourage as many people as fit into the sampling plan to answer the survey. Though many organizations hope to achieve return rates of 80-90%, it is unrealistic to believe this will happen on its own. Just wishing that it will happen won't get you any returned surveys. We have achieved return rates of 97% by 1) making the survey part of a well-organized, well publicized change effort, 2) encouragement by senior management to answer the survey, 3) mandating employees to attend meetings where they have the choice of answering the survey, or turning in a blank one. Without all of these factors, expect at best a 30-40% return rate.

Factor Analyze the Results, Group Items Into Categories and Test Their Reliability.

Factor analysis is a technique most survey authors are not aware of, yet it's a critical and necessary part of survey design. Factor analysis groups items into categories so that it maximizes the reliability and 'sturdiness' of the survey.

The first thing factor analysis does is define how many groups or categories of items to use. No matter how much experience authors may have with developing surveys, how they lump together items into categories often has little relation to the results of factor analysis. The grouping that you have performed is based in part on how a survey author perceives the relationships between survey questions. It is a good method to develop survey questions, but not to develop reliable categories.

What factor analysis does is to, 1) define how many statistically sound categories exist, and, 2) group survey questions into categories based upon the statistical inter-correlations between the questions based on how all survey respondents answered your questionnaire.

This statistical procedure is available through a number of statistics programs, such as SPSS, SAS, NCSS and others. I strongly suggest that you have a good understanding of how factor analysis works before you really have to do it on a short timeline.

After factor-analyzing the survey, test its reliability. Reliability is a measure of how consistently employees answer questions. There are two basic measures of reliability: internal consistency and test-retest. Internal consistency (measured by 'coefficient alpha') measures how well individual questions within each category measure the same thing. Test-retest reliability measures the consistency of survey answers over time. Both are important, but usually coefficient alpha is the only one used. Measuring test-retest reliability would require giving the same survey to the same people again, usually a couple of weeks later. Most survey authors don't want to take the time or effort to do this. However, if measuring organizational change over time, it is a good idea to know how much variation is owing to organizational change and how much is owing to the fuzziness of the questions.

Analyze and Graph the Data.

Now comes the really fun part - analyzing the data. Two of the most common mistakes are, 1) not deciding how you want the graphs to look before you analyze the data, and 2) using survey norms inappropriately.

Imagine yourself with an immense pile of printouts with no idea of how to analyze this data. It is not a fun feeling, believe me. Many a would-be survey analyst has been caught in this problem. The easiest way around this is to decide how to graph and categorize the data to look before this huge ocean of information drowns you.

The easiest way of doing this is to draw a few graphs of how the data might look. Develop a few scenarios with this fake information and ask yourself some questions. "If the data looked this way, what would that mean?" "If the data looks that way, what would that mean?"

Using survey norms inappropriately is another problem. Survey norms are averages of how other people have answered the survey. Established survey companies often use these norms. When you get reports back from them, they will describe how your results stack up against these averages.

There are two problems with this: 1) what norms to use; and 2) how to interpret the numbers. To properly use norms, they must come from an employee population extremely close to yours. This means they should come from the same industry, the same geographic location, the same job types, and the same size of company. Very, very few if any norms exist broken down this finely. To avoid comparing their apples with your oranges, use your own company as a reference point instead of using over-generalized norms. Do this by taking a baseline survey of your employees before (or just at the beginning of) your organizational change effort. Then, re-survey a representative, statistically valid sample of them frequently over time. Compare these later results with your baseline without the problems associated with using someone else's norms.

If you do decide to use these over-generalized norms, remember that people often abuse them in the following way. Let's say that according to these norms, a particular supervisor is in the 20th percentile of listening skills; that is, compared to the norms, 80% scored higher than she did. You automatically conclude that this supervisor has problems with listening skills. This is a bad conclusion taken from faulty data. This is because you are not comparing this supervisor to those in the same industry, geographic location, size of company and so on.

Forget All This Stuff. I'll Just Buy a Survey or Use What We Have.

If you find a survey you like, you can skip all this survey development stuff. The job then focuses on making sure that the purchased survey has followed the above steps. In some cases they have, but often many of these steps are either unknown or ignored by the developers of commercial surveys.

Ask these developers about how and if they use norms, what kinds of reliability measures they use, and what those measures tell them. Ask them if a factor analysis has been done, and what the results are. If they don't understand the questions, they probably don't know their stuff.

Another option is to customize a survey you've already bought. Guess what: customizing an existing survey still requires all of the above steps. Even changing the sequence of questions has a significant effect on reliability.

All this may seem too much to you. If it does, then let me ask you a question: What is the consequence of a wrong organizational decision? If it is severe, then you have little choice then to make organizational changes based on the best information possible. If the consequences of what you are doing are small, why are you going through this tremendous effort of surveying your employees?

Focus: Organization

4

ASSESSING AND IMPROVING YOUR ORGANIZATION: SYMPTOMS, DIAGNOSIS, AND CURES

Almost all of us have belonged to some sick organization at one time or another and at times all of us feel frustrated with them. Unfortunately, many of us are untrained in diagnosing what is going wrong in an organization. All we know is that it isn't working well...

To properly diagnose what is happening in an organization, we start like a doctor — with symptoms. Once we can describe what is going wrong, we look for causes and can then recommend a prescription for what ails the organization.

The assessment process has four steps as described below: 1) get started, 2) assess, 3) choose treatments and use them, and 4) periodically evaluate.

1) Get Started

As in any situation, the first step is to recognize that a problem exists. Doctors call them symptoms. Organizations call them problems. Consultants call them opportunities. These issues can range from declining productivity, quality or market share; dropped, disappearing projects that start marvelously but end up in a black hole; increased absenteeism or turnover; group-related problems; many redundancies and inefficiencies in processes; poorly run meetings; and frequent head-on collisions of style and priorities among management.

If 1) the symptoms outlined above strike home with you, and 2) your senior staff recognizes that these are serious enough problems to warrant investing time and resources; the next step is to decide what actions and resources are needed to diagnose and fix the problem *(steps two through four)*.

At this point, people (as patients) and organizations (as clients) often diagnose themselves and take over-the-counter medications. Organizations take the equivalent: a few people go to a seminar and put on some training programs when they come back. *This works only if you want symptomatic relief!*

Organizations often go through the above process many times, and for awhile they feel better. Unfortunately the underlying causes haven't been assessed and dealt with, so the problem won't go away. Employees in organizations at this time get disease, programitis. Programitis is the feeling of cynicism and indifference that set the tone when organizations plant different buzzwords into the minds of employees without following through on implementation. After a few cycles, the employees expect nothing from management. The initial enthusiasm they have drains away.

Certainly the behavioral changes needed for teamwork must be made by employees and their management. In other words, the patient has to take his medicine. However, resources may be needed outside the organization to objectively assess the patient's health, provide guidance on treatment options and encourage the patient when he is feeling down. Outside resources are especially indicated when previous attempts by management to solve the problem either failed to work or worked only for a short time. These well-intentioned but short-lived solutions might include firing or transferring individual team members, training some of the team in meeting management skills, or browbeating/castigating the team.

Whoever this outside resource may be, he or she should be politically neutral, knowledgeable in team assessment, and able to provide guidance on the many treatment options. This person might be from another division, from a sister company, or from a professional consulting firm. This person should speak frankly, and communicate the problems that your employees feel but are hesitant to talk about.

2) Assess Breadth of the Problem and Identify Causes

Via surveys, interviews and focus groups, determine the breadth and depth of your organizational symptoms. The breadth of organizational illness can be divided into three categories:

Symptoms within just a few groups. These conditions generally involve the goals, roles and relationships in the team. The team's charter or purpose may be vague, or in conflict with group members (or their department's) priorities. The leadership of the group may require feedback and coaching on their management style. Issues of who gets to do what, of group membership, poor group skills and personality conflicts are also potential causes. For further discussion on this, see *'Diagnosing Teamwork Problems'*.

Symptoms between and within groups. Specific issues can arise between teams that create negative effects inside those teams. Such issues include disagreement over responsibilities, allocation of scarce resources, struggles for political power and the like. A typical triangle of conflict is between Marketing, Engineering and Manufacturing.

Symptoms across most of your organization. If illness is prevalent in your company, it implies that organizational systems are a primary cause of the symptoms. Organizational systems such as the organizational structure, compensation, management style, performance appraisal, employee selection process, authority/communication patterns, as well as organizational mission, vision and goals are the major (but often overlooked) causes of organizational ill health. A rule of thumb is that the more widespread the organizational sickness, the greater the likelihood that these systems are causing it.

3) Choose Treatments and Use Them

Treatments for Within-Group Problems
Treatments for within-group issues include further assessment, role clarification, goal setting and problem solving; individual coaching *(See the 'Three Degrees of 360 Feedback')* or removal of members; training in small group skills; and possibly disbanding the group.

Treatments for Inter-Group Problems
Methods to treat inter-group issues include 1) inter-group teambuilding, where warring departments discuss their conflicts and agree upon solutions, 2) establishing cross-functional teams and matrix organizations to deal with 'bridge' issues that cut across organizational lines, 3) merging or dissolution of the groups.

Treatments for Changing Organization-Wide Systems Issues
Methods to treat organization-wide teamwork problems include changing organizational structure to a more product or customer-based focus and away from the functional stovepipes. Other approaches include instituting gainsharing or profit sharing instead of individual

merit reviews; changing market focus and the organization's strategic plan; and including line workers in the design and development of products. For an example, see *'Case Study: Survey-Based Organizational Change'* later in this section.

4) Periodically Evaluate

Increasing organizational health is not a one-shot effort but is continuous and ongoing. Measures of success (such as reassessing organizational health) should be established, and periodic checkups given at one, three, six and 12 months. If the organization progresses, these checkups can become less frequent; they may be more frequent if organizational health starts to go downhill or if the company faces new challenges.

CASE STUDY:
SURVEY-BASED ORGANIZATIONAL CHANGE

An organization is serious about organizational development when it examines two things: how people are paid and how they are promoted. This chapter describes how one organization changed the way it filled job openings. More importantly, the process of identifying a critical area for improvement -- one that required substantial change -- is a story in its own right. Critical lessons can be learned by observing how this new promotion process was developed and how change was implemented.

Background

As part of its ongoing Six Sigma efforts, a number of employees in this company were designated as facilitators, individuals who, after training, would help their organizations implement Six Sigma. These individuals would assist in the design, development and delivery of this training and acted as consultants to management during Six Sigma implementation.

Initial Decisions by Management

At a meeting with the vice president, his direct reports, two facilitators and Organized Change, several decisions were made:

- ⁕ Employees would be surveyed to determine problems with the highest priority.

- ⁕ Recommendations based on survey data would be completed the month before the annual organizational planning conference. This would allow survey actions to become an integral part of organizational goals and budgets.

⬧ Survey administration, communication about events, and development of recommendations would be accomplished by a design team.

⬧ Members of various power blocks in the organization would be represented on this design team. These power blocks included the vice president, directors, managers, supervisors, and multiple representatives from line employees, engineers, support staff, and the union. Except for the union representatives and the vice president, all members would be elected by their peer groups or by representatives of peer groups.

⬧ The two facilitators and the consultant would lead the process.

⬧ This process and its results would be a major portion of the all-employee presentation to be given every six months.

This process provides a unique opportunity to have employee involvement at the start of organizational change and can influence the strategic processes that significantly influence an organization. Employee involvement, therefore, is not the result of an organizational intervention but is a means to it. You might call this employee involvement by pulling your own bootstraps.

Design Team Selection and Formation

With groups involving a small number of people, i.e., directors and managers, all members of the group were brought together. For larger groups, a random sample of people were taken and these were asked to brainstorm a list of potential representatives, and then evaluate these possible representatives on three criteria: knowledge/name recognition of the person; how often the raters listen to this person; and how well these potential representatives listen to their constituents. The person with the highest overall rating was the person chosen to be a representative. This list of people was communicated to the organization via a memo and was also presented as part of an all-employee meeting that organization members attended.

Design Team Training and Team Building

The design team went through an intensive team building process where they became more familiar with one another, defined goals, and defined group norms. After these sessions, team members received training in organizational development and survey feedback techniques. In addition, team members completed an 'authority matrix' intended to clarify, as a result of the survey data, which actions were possible and which were not. For example, the team decided that data would be kept anonymous; that no one would be fired as a result of accusations made by survey respondents; that restructuring was a possibility; that the organization needed a unifying social event, such as a picnic; and that, if warranted, changes in policies and procedures would be made. The team also received additional training immediately before their problem solving began.

Survey Administration and Analysis

The survey developed by Organized Change was a wide-ranging one, with categories including promotions/rewards, teamwork between groups, concern for people and communication at the organizational level and within-group teamwork; Categories also included management's people skills, management support, and participation in decisions at the group level; and job satisfaction, clarity and challenge at the job level. All 750 people in the organization were invited to take the survey at one hour-long session. More than 97% did so, 66% of the surveys included written comments, and one was returned with more than six pages of writing!

The survey categories with the highest need for change were:

- ⁕ Fairness of promotions and rewards
- ⁕ Human relations
- ⁕ Concern for people
- ⁕ Relations between groups
- ⁕ Organization of work

The survey categories which had the lowest need for change were:

- ⁕ Management's people skills

- ⁕ Consistency of group communication

- ⁕ Burnout

- ⁕ Management's technical competence

- ⁕ Performance expectations by management

These data surprised the design team, as they had expected problems with supervision to be the primary issues. They were also surprised by the vehemence of the written comments, and were shocked at some of the examples of poor human relations. A summary of the survey data was communicated to the organization. Survey data is shown in this graph.

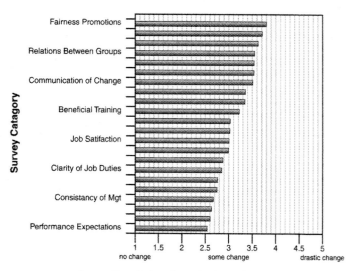

Survey Data Before Organizational Change

Design Team Problem Solving

The team then received eight hours of training in problem solving, training which included brainstorming, cause-effect analysis and criteria rating. Afterward the design team spent 4-1/2 days in problem solving using the survey data as a basis. This was an intense time for the team, but the team building that had been accomplished now allowed members as diverse as a vice president and a clerk to work together, doing so without fear of one another or of suggesting one's ideas. Needless to say, it was an enjoyable but exhausting experience.

Design Team Recommendations

As might be guessed by the breadth of issues, design team recommendations were equally diverse. Some examples include:

- Changing the process to fill open job requisitions

- Developing a management and technical career track based on job analysis

- Establishing bulletin boards for communication

- Creating "surge capacity tiger teams" to minimize work disruptions during times of heavy workload, and

- Establishing a process to recognize well-performing individuals and teams. Not only were these recommendations developed, but communication plans and implementations steps were also defined.

Incorporation Into the Business Cycle

These recommendations were presented at the organization's annual planning conference where goals, objectives and budgets were developed. Most recommendations were approved, funded and implemented. Plans were also developed to communicate these approved recommendations to the rest of the organization, and to re-survey the organization the following year.

The Data, Results and Evaluation

The survey category with the highest need for change was "fairness of promotions and rewards." In response to the survey, the design team made a number of recommendations, one of which dealt with the process of filling job requisitions.

The Old Promotion Process

The old way can best be described as, "It's not what you know, it's who you know." After a manager has justified the need for a job requisition, the paperwork was given to Human Resources. If the manager knew of no one who could fill the position, it sometimes went outside the company with no internal posting. On occasion, the requisition was sent to Human Resources with the name of the person the manager wanted already typed in. Frequently, candidates who interviewed for (but did not fill) the position were never officially told that they weren't hired. They also rarely received feedback as to why they were not qualified nor what they could do to become a better candidate next time.

Implementation and Evaluation

In light of the deficiencies of the old process and the high need for change felt by employees, the design team developed a new process:

- Posting all requisitions for 10 working days.

- Providing verbal and written feedback to all employees interested in the position, including information on what they can do to become more qualified in the future.

- Applying the process to all requisitions below the level of vice president.

- Choosing the winning candidate by a selection committee composed of the head of the group with the requisition; his/her manager; a design team member; and a representative holding the same job classification as the requisition and chosen by his/her peers. In addition, for technical positions, a second peer was chosen. For management positions, a subordinate was chosen by other subordinates to represent their interests.

In this way, employees have influence in choosing their supervisor or manager.

* Using standardized selection criteria across all positions.

* Reviewing the selection process every six months.

Selection Criteria

When designing this process, the design team had to strike a balance between 1) standardizing the criteria for selection, and 2) responding to the unique characteristics of each job. In response, the following was decided:

Jobs were to be divided into three categories: technical (mostly engineering oriented); administrative (clerks and secretaries); and management (supervisors, managers and directors). A list of job criteria (*see the Weighting Matrix*) was developed and applied to these job types. While all criteria were used for all job types, the significance (weighting) differed according to the job. For example, management positions were weighted more heavily by communication and listening skills as well as by the style of participation. Technical positions were weighted more toward versatility/innovation and problem-solving skills than were the administrative or management positions.

Job Type		Past performance	Subject matter knowledge	Analytical/ problem solving skills	Versatility, innovation	Verbal, written communication	Listening skills	Participative style	Customer interface
	Technical	2	3	3	3	2	2	2	2
	Administrative	2	3	2	1	2	2	1	2
	Management	3	2	2	2	3	3	3	3

Weighting Matrix for Selecting Employees to Fill Open Positions

The Process Itself

1) After the requisition was approved, the manager requiring the position (called the requestor) would provide job information (job title, salary grade, exempt/non-exempt status, person reporting to, location) to the design team. This information would be posted on 27 bulletin boards for 10 days. After the 10-day posting period, the requestor and a representative from Human Resources would review the applications filled out by interested employees. The purpose of this review is to select the most qualified candidates for review by the selection committee. All employees applying for the position would receive a telephone call telling them of their status. This would be followed up by a letter confirming the phone conversation, and listing possible avenues for personal development. All non-qualifying candidates would receive feedback before the selection process advanced.

2) The requestor and a design team member would then call meetings of the various groups to be represented on the selection committee. After these groups selected their representatives, the selection committee would receive training in the selection process and be provided guidelines on what kinds of questions are legally allowed. The selection committee would then meet to discuss the scheduling of interviews and to define what questions will be asked of the candidates.

3) Candidates would then be interviewed by the group as a whole. After each interview, the selection committee would discuss the merits of that candidate and rate him/her on the selection criteria, using a 1 to 5 scale. These scale values would then be multiplied by the weights given in the weighting matrix. After all candidates were interviewed, their scores were summed. The candidate with the highest number of points was the person selected to fill the position. If candidates' scores were especially close, the committee would discuss the situation and choose the winning candidate. EEO/affirmative action guidelines were a part of this discussion.

4) All candidates were informed as to the decision and given suggestions (in writing) for personal development.

Post-Intervention Results

As can be seen in the accompanying graph, all survey categories showed a measurably smaller need for change than compared to the year before. This showed a .3 point decline in all survey categories in the (average) need for change perceived by employees. It's difficult to assess whether this was owing to the design team's activities (the selection process, bulletin boards, all-hands meetings, and other actions) or to some other factor. Even so, it's nice to see the numbers go in the right direction.

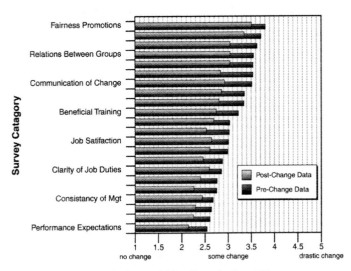

Survey Data Before and After Organizational Changes

Recommendations

Like an onion, peeling away layers of organizational change often reveals more opportunities. Though the selection process has been substantially enhanced, much more work needs to be done to institute fair and equal job opportunities for all. Some recommendations are provided on the next page.

Repeat the process, not the results
The first and strongest recommendation is not to merely copy this selection process wholesale. This process was developed based on a specific need communicated by employees and driven by the previously poor selection process in effect. Your organization may have substantially different needs, and using this process might be using a screwdriver when you need a hammer.

EEO/affirmative action
With the onset of a significant market decline, the number of new positions available was too few to statistically assess whether affirmative action guidelines were affected. If your organization must deal with these considerations, your selection process must be evaluated on these guidelines.

Job descriptions/career ladder
A fundamental, more structural recommendation has to do with career ladders. Not only were job descriptions old and inappropriate, a career ladder among the jobs never existed. As a result, employees were unsure whether or not they had the necessary qualifications for a position. This also made standardizing of interview questions and other selection methods (paper-and-pencil tests, in-baskets, computer simulations) difficult to accomplish. This lack of career ladders also makes it difficult for an employee to incrementally build on his/her skills to achieve a career objective.

Evaluation of selection criteria
Lastly, the selection criteria and their weighting should be evaluated. In general, we all probably agree that management needs greater people skills than technical skills — but to what degree, and how should those skills be reliably tested?

FOCUS: TEAMS

6

DIAGNOSING TEAM PROBLEMS

Almost all of us belong in some form of team, and at times all of us feel frustrated with the team. Unfortunately, few are trained in diagnosing what is going wrong. Although there already has been a chapter on *'Assessing and Improving Your Organization,'* team-related problems have their own particular issues and causes, as described in this chapter.

As in assessing organizations, we start with symptoms. Once we can describe what is going wrong, we look for causes and recommend a prescription for what ails us. The first part of this chapter deals with symptoms; the second with causes; and the third with prescriptions for what ails the teams.

Is that sick feeling from the Stewed Tomato Surprise you had last night, or from that disastrous meeting this morning?

Symptoms

Drops, Plops, Pinches, and Abilenes
One symptom to look for is perhaps the most obvious: a drop in productivity or quality. If a group has had a sudden drop in productivity, or a gradual decline over time, it usually means a team's ability to get along is either a cause or is suffering as well. Imagine this situation:

> A manager is called into her director's office. This guy has her group's productivity charts on the wall and these show a bumpy but significant decline. He blasts her group, asking her who the problem is, suggesting that if she doesn't shape up soon he will find another manager for the group. "Someone," he says, "to make the tough decisions." This was not the first time he had acted this way. He had said things like this to all group members.

Relations within the group have deteriorated as well. What previously was cooperation and hard work has turned into competition and blame. What the director did not realize is that he was the initial cause of the group's decline in productivity. Instead of encouraging the group and giving them the help they needed, he looked for a scapegoat. This negative behavior caused bad feelings in the group, which in turn caused the group's productivity to decline further, all of which, by the way, made the director angrier than ever. These kind of vicious cycles are often recognized by outsiders but rarely noticed by those caught up in them.

Plops happen when some usually quiet or new member brings up an idea or concern, and the reaction is deadly silence. Perhaps their idea touched a sacred cow, or maybe they have low status in the group. This happens occasionally in any group, but if it consistently happens when a topic is brought up, or consistently to one person, it sends the message that new ideas are unwelcome and that people should "keep their place." This stifling of ideas cuts off creativity from all but a powerful few.

Pinches are the hurt feelings and frustrations that members feel when their expectations aren't met. Perhaps they didn't get on the project they wanted to, their roles are not as powerful as they wished, they didn't agree with the orders from on high, or management said one thing and did something else. In groups without open communication, these pinches accumulate until finally there comes a 'crunch.' Crunches can be emotional blowups on trivial decisions, people leaving the group, and tasks being sabotaged. Unfortunately if groups ignore pinches, they ignore crunches too: After an awkward silence, someone moves the topic to a different subject, cracks a joke, or suggests the meeting be adjourned. Because these pinches and crunches aren't dealt with, they will occur more frequently. One of the more nasty pinches is the blaming of other people for failure.

Dr. Jerry Harvey tells about his family who went to Abilene, Texas. Called the Abilene Paradox, family members thought everyone else wanted to go there, even though they personally did not. More generally, groups often undertake actions and achieve progress on goals on which no group member agreed. This problem occurs when group members poorly communicate their wishes and are not encouraged to do so. The group also may have no open forum for creating a consensus. As a result, the group can devote significant time and effort to something that serves no purpose. As described in Dr. Harvey's book, this lack of communication and false assumptions about goals and objectives can lead to much wasted time and effort.

Draggers, Assassins, and the G.T.s

How agreement is managed is often the stickiest point in group life. All of a group's strengths, weaknesses and foibles come together whenever a decision needs to be made.

Imagine this:

> The group had been meeting for two hours every week for the last month. No one really seemed to have a handle on the problem, much less an answer. George Godzilla suddenly raises his voice and says, "I'm tired of all this talk. We keep going around in circles. We need to do something now! I say we just reduce everybody's budget by 10%. That ought to get them off of our back. " After about 10 seconds, some in the group nod yes, and George says, "All right, it's agreed then. Turn in your budgets by Monday 7 a.m." Signs of either disquiet or relief come from the rest of the group. This sign of dominance by a few members reduces participation by others, stifles new ideas, and creates the illusion of consensus. The group is dragged along by a few powerful, vocal advocates. Without full consensus, commitment to the decision will not be there and people will tend to miss deadlines, 'forget' tasks, and may deliberately block others' actions. When the leader of the group is one of the draggers, it sends signals to others that this is acceptable behavior in the groups they lead.

Not all groups are even this open. Cliques inside groups are formed, advancing their ideas at the expense of others. There are plots, assassins, coups and counter-coups. To some extent this happens in all groups, but the problem comes when the victory of one clique comes at the expense of the whole group, or even the whole organization. This 'sub-optimizing' with its veil of smiles and nodding of heads can destroy group health more subtly than any attack by competitors or by a decline in productivity.

The G.T.s, or *groupthink*, is an embarrassing symptom for a group to have. It's like bad breath: Everyone else knows you have it except you. Groupthink is where group members feel invulnerable to error, rarely admit to mistakes, and actively discourage disagreement among themselves and others. This blindness, as described by Dr. Irving Janis, led to such wonderful decisions as Chamberlain's appeasement of Hitler, the Bay of Pigs invasion of Cuba, and Johnson's escalation of the war in Vietnam. Groups often do not realize that they have these symptoms because admitting this would contradict the invulnerability they feel. Most likely groupthink occurred during Board and Audit Committee meetings that put so many companies under the cloud of accounting scandal.

Causes

Now that you are a complete hypochondriac, let's talk about causes of these symptoms.

Goals, Roles, and Relationships

Much of the trouble people have from groups comes either from assumptions about what goals, roles, and relationships should be in a group, or about what agreement exists on these topics.

The usual problem with goals is that they are not specific enough. Such goals as "reduce costs by 10%," "improve quality," and "develop a better attitude" may be good to hear but are meaningless until we agree on what costs, what measure of quality, and what behaviors constitute an attitude.

Roles play a complex part in how a group functions. First of all, roles have to do with who will do what task. Let's face it — some tasks give us more exposure to the big bosses, others let us appear to be working hard, and yet others are tasks we would never do but would delegate to others.

Secondly, roles deal with power. Roles define who can make what decisions, with or without someone else's OK, who we have to report to, and those whom we can safely ignore. Power is the central issue in participative management, self-directed work groups, and employee involvement efforts.

One example of role confusion happened with the staff of a vice president who was considering reorganization. The staff believed they were empowered to make changes and that barring any significant technical problems, the vice president would go along with these changes. In this light, they proceeded to remove supervisors from their organizations and replaced them with 'team leaders.' In addition, they removed one organization from directly reporting to the vice president. When it came time to present the new organization charts, the vice president disagreed and stated that neither of these actions would be put into effect. Stunned silence ensued. Authority had not been discussed beforehand: they assumed one role; the vice president assumed another.

Thirdly, roles have to do with behavior. Who will play the jokester, and who the heavy? Who is perpetually typecast, and who is mercurial and a 'loose cannon?' Is the manager good at giving feedback and encouraging group members to contribute?

These goals and roles play a significant role in how we deal with others in the group. When we agree with someone on what these goals and roles should be, that individual becomes part of our clique; if not, he or she may become an enemy. Our experience with group members outside the group and in the past combines with these goals and roles to create 'personality' conflicts, sharp clashes of opinion, or, in well functioning groups, greater effectiveness and creativity. These actions then influence the goals and roles in the group.

The Systems Viewpoint and the Bigger Picture

As with a patient, a group's surroundings and interactions with others can greatly affect whether we contract a disease, whether we recognize it, and how quickly we recover from it. With groups, the organization they are a part of plays that role. Such factors as performance appraisals encourage individual achievement or teamwork; and whether groups are financially rewarded instead of individuals can either reinforce or tear apart a group's attempt at teamwork.

Suppose employees whose loyalties and rewards are tied to their 'functional stovepipes' (Finance, Production, Human Resources, etc.) are thrown together onto a team supposed to reduce waste across your organization. Do you seriously think their chances of success are great when major sacrifices by their own functions are necessary? Wouldn't their ideas to eliminate these stovepipes be quashed by the very people who gave them the task? As all of you know, one of the most frustrating things is to be given responsibility without authority.

The information system surrounding the group also has a significant effect. The natural flows of information come from the organizational structure of which it is a part, from the computer system that partly delivers it, and from the friendships and other relationships that are formed over time. If the information system does not allow people to collaborate effectively, they will continue to remain isolated despite the best organizational charts and teambuilding available.

In summary, to really find out what is causing teamwork problems, use a systems perspective as shown in the accompanying diagram. Factors that are both inside and outside the team can either block or enhance teamwork. How well they work together is up to the team and the management that supports them.

7

CASE STUDY: HOW NOT TO USE A TEAM

A client contacted Organized Change and asked for help with a quality improvement team that "just wasn't producing results." This organization provided vital equipment to their customers, was the major supplier of this product to Motorola and Texas Instruments, and was quite profitable. They had been audited by these firms with positive results. Despite all this, why couldn't they make effective use of one quality team?

The company has three product lines, two of which concern us here. They manufacture 'product A' which is a generic piece of chip testing equipment. They also make 'product B' which is a set of materials and equipment ('custom packages') that allows their customer to insert chips into product A for testing. Depending on the exact type of chip to be tested, there are many variations of product B.

Company management formed a quality team to improve the process of engineering, manufacturing and assembling product B because 1) some customers complained of not receiving the right custom packages on time; and 2) significant production problems arose even when making fairly simple packages.

Management formed the team by taking middle-management members from manufacturing, engineering, sales, service, and accounting. Management offered to pay for training in a variety of total quality subjects. A number of group members took this training.

The team met from 2-4 hours a week with participation by all in almost all the meetings. They conducted their meetings during work hours and these were held in addition to their 60-80 hour work weeks. They'd worked this way for a year before senior management called us in.

How We Collected Our Data

We used a variety of ways to collect data: we observed the team in action, took a look at the production floor, interviewed senior management and the team, and asked the team to take a standardized survey we use to determine the group dynamics of cross-functional teams. The survey included 48 numerical items answered on a need-for-change scale (1= needs no change, 2= needs a little change, 3= needs some change, 4= needs much change, 5= needs drastic change). and we used three open-ended questions to obtain more in-depth information. The 48 questions were part of eight survey categories:

* *Group effectiveness.* Measuring the perceived effectiveness of the group.

* *Communication comfort/assertiveness.* Willingness of group members to communicate their opinions.

* *Mutual influence.* How well members influence each other.

* *Personal involvement.* How much interest members have in working in the group.

* *Intra-group trust.* How much group members support and trust one another.

* *Submission vs rebellion against group leader.* How willingly are members going to follow the group leader.

* *Role and idea conformity.* How comfortable and effective do members feel about the roles they perform.

Results of Data Collection

In summary, we found the team to be frustrated, angry and burned out. As shown in the following graph, the survey categories with the highest need for change include intragroup trust and group effectiveness. Agenda setting/meeting content and role and idea conformity (how much members feel comfortable and effective in the roles they perform) were also moderately high. Based on the team interviews, the need for change is probably higher that what the graph shows. Burnout and excessive fatigue can cause this.

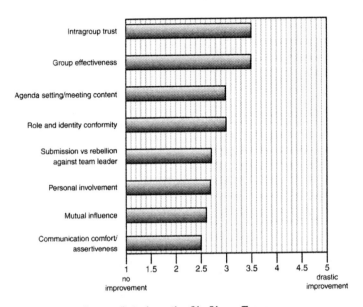

Survey Data from the Six Sigma Team

'Spontaneous combustion' occurred at several meetings with many members shouting angrily at each other. Group members during the interviews acted as if they once were interested in solving this problem but now were just slogging through the mud hoping to see dawn and an end to their journey. Team members felt a tremendous lack of support by management and regarded management's attempts at support as unwelcome, uninformed browbeatings.

Senior management was not especially happy, either. They had provided training and time to this group, apparently with no results. When senior management tried to help by attending meetings, they were rebuffed. To me it sounded like a couple who just had an argument, with each spouse pouting in a corner waiting for the other to apologize.

What Went Wrong?

On the basis of our surveys, interviews and observations, we discovered many causes to this team's difficulties:

Causes outside the group.

> ⁕ *A nonexistent measurement system.* The company did not track accurately, consistently or completely the quality defects and on-time delivery. As a result of this, management's desire to improve quality was based on anecdotal customer complaints and not on data collection.

> ⁕ *A nonexistent charter.* Management did not provide clear direction to the group as to its purpose, its expected results, the methods to use, or a timetable for completion.

> ⁕ *Lack of management involvement from the start.* Management became involved only when they thought the team was in trouble and was not performing to their un-communicated expectations. They were always 'cc' on memos and the team made several attempts at making presentations. However, management still did not think they were well informed about the team's activities.

> ⁕ *Management not knowing how to support the team.* I came to the conclusion that management was willing to help but did not know how. They acted as if they thought that the team was a wind-up toy to be wound up at the beginning and then let go.

> ⁕ *An ill-suited organizational structure that worked against the team.* The company was organized along traditional functional lines into Manufacturing, Engineering, Sales, Service, and Human Resources. This meant that the company had no "process owners" who took care of products A, B and C. Because of this, the team did not have any person to go to who was in charge of product B.

® *Poor scheduling of production.* The company used a home-made collection of spreadsheets to manage a rapidly changing production environment. To make scheduling more complex, manufacturing product B required short, low-volume runs -- something that is hard to schedule no matter what software you have.

® *No incentive to improve the process.* Management had in place a traditional pay structure, with no monetary or other incentive in place to improve customer satisfaction, efficiency or profitability.

Causes inside the group:

® *A poor measurement system.* Unfortunately, the group took six months to develop and start tracking defects in product B. To add to this, the measurement system they developed included only the defects in one part of their machine shop and excluded defects found by customers and during assembly of the parts.

® *No 'up-front' teambuilding.* No one conducted activities to help the team members become familiar with each other, to clarify the charter, to define roles and expectations or to develop group norms and groundrules.

® *The wrong people in the team.* Most major functions had a representative in the group, but Engineering had two where only one was needed. Accounting was part of the team, but had little need to be there. Her lack of technical expertise slowed-down team conversations, and required other team members to spend considerable meeting time bringing her up to speed.

® *Inconsistent training.* Some members attended some seminars, while other group members attended different ones. Yet other members did not attend at all. In one case, one member attended a seminar on process mapping while a second member attended a different seminar on the same topic. Both of them tried to assist the team by applying the techniques they'd just learned. Unfortunately, however, after much discussion and confusion they realized that although they were using the same terms these terms had different personal meanings.

❋ *Authority-responsibility mismatch.* A quality improvement team works best when it has a clearly defined, specific problem that they solve or prevent from happening again and then disappear. Unfortunately, this quality team had the responsibility to continually run a production line without management authority to do so.

Recommendations

We recommended the following:

1) *Install a proper production scheduling system.* Without a system such as Material Requirements Planning (MRP) or the like, there is almost no way that customers can get what they need on time.

2) *Management must choose one of the three following options:*
   ❋ *Disband the team.* They have been given too much to do with too little authority, and were close to burnout.

   ❋ *Reduce the scope of the team to a specific problem and change the membership accordingly.* This would make the group a true quality improvement team, with management having the overall responsibility of improving product B.

   ❋ *Reorganize the company into separate product lines.* The company had three separate product lines with little overlap. This reorganization would allow the company to focus its resources into each specific product, and would minimize the cross-functional conflict that occurs when companies are organized by functional stovepipes of Manufacturing, Sales, Engineering, and Service. Many companies of this size that have distinct product lines can benefit tremendously from this organizational structure.

FOCUS: IMPROVING LEADERS

8

Giving Feedback on Management Style: The Three Degrees of 360° Feedback

Giving feedback on management style is one of the more difficult tasks of organizational change. For better or worse, changes in mission, organizational structure, pay systems and who gets hired may affect you personally, but the changes are not directly about you. When it comes to receiving feedback on your management style, it not only affects you *personally*, it is *personal*. It's no wonder that despite it's popularity, implementing systems that give feedback on management style must be done with caution given the sensitive nature of the data and the possible defensiveness of the employees who receive it.

Management Style, and a Summary of 360° Feedback

Until the latter 1960s, feedback on management style has usually come from the top down. Either as part of a yearly performance appraisal, or after a particularly disastrous event at the company, a manager has received feedback from his/her boss either as, 1) part of a heated exchange of views just before the manager is fired or, 2) heard vague, uncomfortable mouthings about improving relations with people.

This started to change with the advent of sensitivity groups, or 'T' groups in the 1960s. During these sessions lasting several days, employees from a variety of organizations came together to learn how people felt about each other in a group.

The main focus was on personal growth and development. Because of this focus, employees came back to their workplace intent on acting differently and better towards their fellow employees. Unfortunately, 'T' groups were not successful in the long run because managers returned to the same work environment that either didn't reward the new, more caring behaviors or were overwhelmed by other managers acting the same old way. In response, the various consulting groups and institutes that ran T groups began to focus feedback sessions on work behaviors and management style. Through various exercises, situations and discussions, participant's behaviors were compared to national norms and received counseling and feedback on how to improve.

Starting in the 1980s, a new wrinkle to this approach was developed. As the idea of increasing employee influence and autonomy (employee empowerment) became popular, the thought arose that a manager ought to receive management style feedback from more than one source, from those who knew them best: their subordinates, their boss, their peers, and themselves. This information was usually gathered via numerical surveys and open-ended questionnaires. This feedback from all those in the circle who knew someone became known as '360° feedback.'

Options for Implementation

There are three options for implementing 360° feedback, each more comprehensive and powerful in promoting change, both organizational and personal:

1) Send a few managers to an outside consultancy for assessment and feedback. In this option, managers may hand out surveys to those whom they know (and expect to get feedback from with minimal negative information) the data collected by the consultancy, and the managers, receive an 'offsite' training and feedback session with similar managers from different companies. This approach has been derogatively called "sending the fair-haired boys to charm school."

While this approach has its merits, its major deficiency is the same problem that T groups had: a few individuals are changed, the overwhelming mass of management is not, and the systems and processes that encourage old behaviors are still in place.

2) The second approach is to bring such a program at the organization where many managers receive 360° feedback. In this approach, the feedback can be more systematic for two reasons: 1) surveys are handed out to all subordinates and peers rather than to those who have been 'volunteered' by the person receiving feedback. This tends to reduce the 'sampling bias' of just giving it to

those who might give only good feedback, and 2) the implementation of this process can be from the top of the organization down to the bottom. This has the advantage of allowing upper management to serve as an example of willingly receiving such feedback and thus encouraging upper management to be both models of behavior and coaches to those underneath them.

3) The third approach involves all of the second approach, and also deals with 'systems issues.' Where 360° feedback alone can only deal with problems caused by individual behavior, by itself it does nothing for the systemic causes of problems, such as organizational structure, inappropriate and distorted measurement systems, company-wide lack of skills, or performance appraisal and pay problems. However, 360° feedback can serve both as a catalyst to help management realize the systematic causes of organizational problems, and can be part of the solution so that management style comes into harmony with other organizational changes senior management is trying to make.

Questions to Ask Before You Start

A word of caution here: questions about implementing 360° feedback are easy to ask but not so easy to answer. Often management assumes the answers but does not openly discuss them, the result being much chaos and confusion down the road.

Some of these questions are:

❋ How ready is your organization to handle 360° feedback? Frequently organizations may be willing to pay consultants to assist them in implementing such a system, but the organization needs to be prepared. At times, 'soft skills' training in communication, leadership, management style, meeting management, etc., is useful in preparing management. Teambuilding activities might also be useful, as well as a general organizational climate survey to determine the context of implementation and to find any additional issues beyond management style that might pose a problem.

※ Who needs to agree? Who will be the decision-making body about 360° feedback? Will it be the head of the organization, or Human Resources, or a cross-section of employees from a variety of levels?

※ Who will be involved? Which employees are to be the focus of the 360° feedback, and who will provide it to them?

※ Is this voluntary or mandatory? Will some employees be offered the 'opportunity' to receive this feedback, will everyone receive it, or will only management receive the feedback?

※ What methods and measurements will be used? Will employees just fill out numerical surveys or will this information be supplemented with observations and interviews? Will the report be only a graph, a summary of high need for change survey items, or will there be a written report with recommendations? To what extent will this report be personalized and hand-crafted vs being automated?

※ To what extent will the data be collected anonymously and/or confidentially? While the intent may be to keep the survey data anonymous, if written comments or interview data are also included the data may have to be altered to avoid making obvious conclusions about who communicated what. In addition, management must answer questions about personal, confidential data that might be accidentally revealed during interviews.

※ What will be done with alleged violations of laws, ethics or policies? Though this may not be the intent of 360° feedback, on occasion information is gathered that suggests violations of legal, ethical and company codes of conduct.

❋ What information will be public? At first blush, you might think that all data will be private, but does that mean that one's own supervisor can't see the data and the report? Will group and company averages be made public without them being broken down into individual scores?

❋ What consequences will there be? Will they receive additional coaching and counseling, training, or be terminated or re-assigned? Will the 360° feedback be the sole determining factor of this decision?

❋ What logistics and support will be necessary to make this successful? To what extent will the data be collected electronically (via the Web or intranet) or on paper? What administrative and technical support will be necessary?

❋ What systems changes will accompany this organizational change? As stated earlier, providing feedback on management style in and of itself can only be part of organizational change and can rarely stand on its own. As a result, one must ask how and when 360° feedback will be incorporated into training, selection, and pay decisions?

Summary

We received a phone call from the director of sales from a division of a multi-billion dollar biomedical company. As part of a training and decision-making session with his direct reports, he wanted feedback and training on his and his subordinates' management style.

We had extensive discussions about the content of the survey. In addition to the usual survey questions on listening skills and the support to subordinates, there were questions on consistency of communication, business/clinical knowledge and task management, as well as on sales competencies. We asked open-ended questions on how their management and support behaviors could be improved, and collected the data using both paper-based and electronic methods using our proprietary software, OCSS.

Results of the Data Collection

The data were graphed automatically using OCSS, as an example shows below:

Average of Responses

In addition, the graphs were summarized as the example below shows, with the Xs marking areas needing at least some improvement:

Survey item	Person describing you				
	all	self	sub.	peer	boss
Consistency of communication					
How often this person ...					X
How often this person ...					
Functional competencies - knowledge and development					
The degree of ...				X	X
This person's knowledge ...				X	
How well this person...				X	
How much this person					
How well this person...					
Functional competencies - selling and economics					X
This person's ability to ...					X
This person's ...				X	X
This person's ...					X

Feedback to the Head of the Group

We also developed a one-page summary of the data plus our recommendations to the head of the group, as shown below:

The Short And The Sweet For "John Boss"

Summary of issues

- ❋ Buy in by subordinates and other functions

- ❋ Consistency in direction, changing lanes too fast

- ❋ Delegation of authority

You seem to move at a rapid pace, a necessity for someone with a heavy workload and who tries to take advantage of opportunities that appear and disappear overnight. However, this pressure for speed can leave behind some of those you should take with you - your subordinates and other departments.

Recommendations

* Obtain input from those around you, including subordinates and peers when appropriate. Slow down your pace of talking, especially when giving a change in directions. Evaluate your decisions as to their "whipsaw" effect on your subordinates and your peers.

* Consider, on a person by person basis, whether you can delegate greater authority in decision-making, rather than just handing them a problem. For those who are less assertive than you, encourage opportunities to disagree with you, and give them the time to do so.

* Consider what actions you need to take to "systematize" the process you have developed so that is it not so dependent on individual coaching. Make the process scaleable, so that the system can be expanded without strain when the organization grows.

Feedback to individuals

The issues raised about individual subordinates were quite varied. An example is shown below:

The Short And The Sweet For Bruce Subordinate

Summary of issues

- You listen well, when you listen

- Focus on the immediate problem rather than on the next one

- Selling skills

- Industry knowledge, dealing with young team

Recommendations

- Apply your excellent listening skills to the current situation. There may be some body language or para-language behaviors (voice intonation, inflection, etc.) that are giving people the impression you are not listening to the current issue at hand, and instead are focusing on the next concern.

- Develop your selling and clinical knowledge skills in yourself, but especially among your inexperienced subordinates.

Feedback to the Group as a Whole: What was Missing and What Needed to be Done

One of the surprising findings to us was how little the organization was considering the future. While the organization had adequate methods to develop its employees for the current situation, it had hardly prepared them for the future. Though the division was competing against new companies, preparing to sell a more diversified line of products, and hiring a significant number of new employees, it gave little thought to how its hiring and training practices should change.

The current method of training sales personnel relied almost exclusively on one-on-one coaching and company-provided technical material. Although this was adequate for a one- or two-layer organization, using these methods alone would be inadequate for an expanding staff. We recommended that the organization review its criteria for new hires, with special emphasis on their experience and ability to sell many products; add e-learning to their training mix to provide the continuous availability of learning materials to a traveling workforce; begin using collaborative tools for increased capability beyond conference calls; and, since the current sales force will become managers of others, develop a leadership training program to prepare this sales team for its new role.

As a result of this missing element, we developed a "visioning" exercise for the sales force, asking them to describe the situation and circumstances that might arise three years from now. Though this method is not as complete as the scenario planning methods described in my other book, No More Darn Buzzwords: Keys to Successful Organized Change, it did provide the participants with a great deal of food for thought. They came to realize what was going to be necessary in their new, more competitive environment.

ACKNOWLEDGEMENTS AND SUGGESTED READINGS

Jack Edwards, Maria Thomas, Paul Rosenfeld and Stephanie Booth-Kewley (1996) How to conduct organizational surveys. Sage Publications.

Paul S. Goodman & Associates. (1986). Designing Effective Work Groups.

Jerry Harvey. (1996). The Abilene Paradox and Other Meditations on Management.

William Hayes (1973). Statistics for the social sciences. 2nd edition. New York: Holt, Rineheart and Winston, Inc.

Jerry Hitnze (1995). Number Cruncher Statistical System User's Guide. Kaysville, UT:NCSS, pages 1149-1158.

Irving Janis and Leon Mann. (1977). Decision Making.

Graham Kalton (1983). Introduction to survey sampling. Sage Series in Quantitative Applications in the Social Sciences, number 07-035. Newbury Park, CA: Sage Publications.

Robert Kaplan and David Norton (1996). The balanced scorecard.

Robert Kaplan and David Norton (2001). The Strategy-Focused Organization.

Roger Kirk(1968). Experimental design: procedures for the behavioral sciences. Belmont, CA: Brooks/Cole.

William Klecka (1980). Discriminant Analysis. Sage Series in Quantitative Applications in the Social Sciences, number 07-019. Newbury Park, CA: Sage Publications.

William Lee and Diana Owens (2000). Multimedia-based Instructional Design.

My thanks to M. David Merrill, Ph.D. for developing the 'component-display' matrix for classifying training objectives.

Jack Orburn, Linda Moran, Ed Musselwhite & John Zenter (1990). Self-Directed Work Teams: The New American Challenge.

George Piskurich. (2000). Rapid Instructional Design.

Charles Reigluth (1999). Instructional-Design Theories and Models: A New Paradigm of Instructional Theory.

William Rothwell (2001). Effective Succession Planning.

Peter Schartz(2004). Inevitable surprises: Thinking ahead in a time of turbulence.

Marvin Shaw (1971). Group Dynamics.

The story of the rich man going to a monastery was adapted from The Gospel According to Zen, edited by Robert Sohl and Audrey Carr (1970).